Disclaimers

1. The information in this book is intended to assist in planning and leading safety meetings and is not a substitute for professional advice or consultation.

2. The tips and suggestions in this book are based on general safety principles and may not apply to every situation or industry.

3. The author and publisher of this book are not responsible for any errors or omissions or any actions taken based on the information provided in this book.

4. The author and publisher of this book do not assume any liability for any loss or damage that may result from the use of this book, including but not limited to direct, indirect, incidental, or consequential damages.

5. The information in this book is subject to change without notice and may not be updated after publication.

6. The author and publisher of this book make no guarantees or warranties, express or implied, regarding the accuracy, completeness, reliability, suitability, or availability of the information contained in this book.

7. It is the reader's responsibility to evaluate the accuracy, completeness, and usefulness of any information provided in this book and to seek professional advice as necessary.

8. The safety tips and suggestions in this book are not intended to replace or override any safety regulations or policies established by an organization or government agency.

9. The safety tips and suggestions in this book are intended to supplement existing safety programs and practices rather than as a replacement for them.

10. Safety isn't expensive, it's priceless. -Unknown

<u>Introduction</u>

Safety is an essential aspect of any workplace and should be a top priority for all business owners and safety professionals. The safety of employees, customers, and visitors must always be considered when making decisions and taking action. However, with so many safety topics to cover, it can be overwhelming to know where to begin.

This book is designed to help small business owners, safety professionals, and others have a quick and easy guide to lead or plan safety training and meetings. The book contains 10 points on 50 different safety topics, covering a wide range of important safety issues that businesses must address.

Each page in the book focuses on a specific safety topic and provides concise, easy-to-understand information and practical advice on managing and preventing potential hazards. Whether new to safety training or a seasoned safety professional, this book will help you stay up-to-date with the latest safety regulations and best practices.

The information in this book is based on years of experience and research in the safety field. It's been written with the busy schedules of small business owners and safety professionals in mind, so you can quickly access the information you need to keep your workplace safe.

Ultimately, the goal of this book is to provide a valuable resource that can be used to create a culture of safety in any workplace. By implementing the advice and information provided in these pages, you can help ensure the safety of your employees, customers, and visitors and minimize the risk of accidents and injuries.

Topics

1	Accident Investigation
2	Aerial Lift Safety
3	Asbestos Awareness
4	Back Injury Prevention
5	Bomb Threats
6	Carbon Monoxide Poisoning Prevention
7	Chemical Handling & Storage
8	Cleaning Chemical Safety
9	Cold & Flu Prevention
10	Computer Safety
11	Confined Space Entry
12	CPR
13	Crane Safety
14	Cuts & Abrasions Prevention
15	Dealing with Chemical Spills
16	Driving Accident Prevention
17	Dust Hazards
18	Electrical Safety
19	Ergonomics
20	Fatigue Management
21	Fire Prevention
22	First Aid
23	Foot Protection
24	H_2S Safety
25	Hand Injury Prevention

Topics (continued)

26	Hand Tool Safety
27	Hard Hats
28	HazMat Handling and Storage
29	Heat Illness Prevention
30	High Voltage Safety
31	Horseplay at the Workplace
32	Importance of Hydration
33	Job Hazard Analysis
34	Ladder Safety
35	Lockout Tagout
36	Manual Handling and Lifting
37	Medical Emergencies
38	Mobile Equipment Safety
39	Near Miss Reporting
40	Office Safety
41	Personal Protective Equipment
42	Preventing Workplace Violence
43	Respiratory Protection
44	Scaffolding Safety
45	Slips, Trips & Falls
46	Stress Management
47	Trenching Safety
48	Truck & Trailer Safety
49	Winter Driving
50	Workplace Housekeeping

Forms

1	Safety Meeting Sign in Sheet
2	10 Point Safety Talk Notes
3	Items Discussed for Documentation

1. Accident Investigation

1. Accident investigation determines the cause of an accident or incident to prevent similar incidents.

2. The first step in an accident investigation is to secure the accident scene, ensuring that it is safe for investigators to enter.

3. The investigation team should include personnel with expertise in areas related to the accident, such as safety, engineering, and management.

4. The investigation team should also interview witnesses, review documentation, and examine physical evidence to gather information about the accident.

5. The root cause of the accident should be identified, which is the underlying causes and factors rather than just the immediate cause.

6. The investigation team should develop and implement corrective actions to address the root cause of the accident and prevent similar incidents from occurring in the future.

7. Documentation should include the findings of the accident investigation in a report that includes a description of the accident, the root cause, and the corrective actions taken.

8. Management or safety staff should share accident investigation reports with all relevant personnel to improve safety plans.

9. Staff should approach accident investigations with a learning attitude rather than blaming or punishing the individuals involved.

10. Accurate and timely accident investigation is critical for maintaining a safe work environment, preventing future accidents, and reducing the costs associated with accidents.

2. Aerial Lift Safety

1. Aerial lifts are commonly used in construction, maintenance, and other industries to lift workers to elevated workspaces.

2. Aerial lifts should only be operated by trained and authorized personnel who have received appropriate safety training.

3. Workers should always wear appropriate personal protective equipment (PPE) when operating or working on an aerial lift, including a full-body harness and lanyard.

4. Before operating an aerial lift, workers should inspect the equipment for any signs of damage or malfunction, including brakes, steering, and electrical systems.

5. Aerial lifts should only be operated on level surfaces and in stable conditions, with the wheels or outriggers adequately positioned and secured.

6. Workers should always be within the load capacity of the aerial lift and never use it for any purposes other than lifting personnel and equipment to elevated workspaces.

7. Workers should be aware of overhead hazards, such as power lines or tree branches, and maintain a safe distance from them.

8. Workers should never climb on or lean over the guardrails of an aerial lift, as this can cause the lift to tip over.

9. Workers should be aware of weather conditions, including high winds, rain, or ice, that can affect the stability of the aerial lift and take appropriate precautions.

10. Regular maintenance and inspections of aerial lifts are essential for ensuring their safe operation and preventing accidents.

3. Asbestos Awareness

1. Asbestos is a mineral fiber commonly used in construction materials, such as insulation and ceiling tiles, until many countries banned it due to its health risks.

2. Asbestos exposure can cause serious respiratory illnesses, including lung cancer and mesothelioma, which may not develop until many years after exposure.

3. Workers potentially exposed to asbestos should receive appropriate training and education on the health risks associated with asbestos exposure.

4. Employers should identify and assess potential sources of asbestos at a job site and implement appropriate controls to minimize worker exposure.

5. Workers should always wear appropriate PPE, such as respirators and disposable coveralls, when working with or near asbestos-containing materials.

6. Workers should not eat, drink, or smoke in areas with asbestos, which can increase the risk of inhaling asbestos fibers.

7. Asbestos-containing materials should be appropriately labeled and handled to prevent the release of asbestos fibers into the air.

8. Workers should follow appropriate procedures for handling asbestos-containing debris or materials and avoid disturbing asbestos-containing materials when possible.

9. Safety staff should complete regular monitoring and testing to assess worker exposure to asbestos and ensure adequate control measures.

10. If workers suspect asbestos exposure, they should immediately inform their employer and seek medical attention.

4. Back Injury Prevention

1. Back injuries are common workplace injuries commonly resulting in pain, lost time, or disability.

2. Workers should receive proper training on safe lifting techniques, including how to use equipment to assist in lifting, such as lifting straps or hand trucks.

3. Workers should be encouraged to use proper lifting techniques when lifting heavy or awkward objects, including bending at the knees while keeping the back straight.

4. Employers should provide ergonomic equipment, such as adjustable chairs and desks, to reduce the risk of back injuries caused by poor posture.

5. Workers with jobs that require sitting or standing for extended periods should take frequent breaks to stretch or move.

6. Employers should conduct ergonomic assessments of workstations and job tasks to identify potential risk factors for back injuries.

7. Workers should immediately report any pain or discomfort in their back or other body parts to their employer or supervisor.

8. Employers should document any reports of back injuries; following a report, an employer should follow proper Workers' Compensation and other company procedures.

9. Workers should be encouraged to maintain a healthy lifestyle, including regular exercise and a balanced diet, to reduce the risk of back injuries.

10. Employers should foster a culture of safety where workers feel comfortable reporting safety concerns, and safety is a top priority.

5. Bomb Threats

1. A bomb threat can be made via phone, email, or other means and should always be taken seriously.

2. Workers should be trained on who to notify and what actions to take in the case of a bomb threat.

3. All bomb threats should be reported immediately to the authorities via 911, and any suspicious packages or items should be reported to security or management personnel.

4. Employers should include evacuation procedures and communication protocols in their emergency plans in the case of a bomb threat.

5. Muster locations, in case of a bomb threat, should be communicated to all workers and drills conducted.

6. Workers should be advised to keep their personal belongings with them in the event of an evacuation, as they may be unable to return to the workplace for some time.

7. If an explosion occurs, workers should take cover, protect themselves from debris, and follow emergency procedures for evacuation and medical attention.

8. After a bomb threat or incident, the workplace should be thoroughly searched and cleared by authorities before workers can return.

9. Workers should be reminded not to touch or move suspicious items, as they may be dangerous or contain evidence.

10. Employers should provide support and counseling for workers who may be traumatized by a bomb threat or incident.

6. Carbon Monoxide Poisoning Prevention

1. Carbon monoxide (CO) is a colorless, odorless gas that can be deadly if inhaled in high concentrations.

2. Sources of CO include gas-powered equipment, fuel-burning appliances, and running vehicles in enclosed spaces.

3. Workers should receive training on identifying and preventing CO exposure, including recognizing symptoms of CO poisoning.

4. Employers should ensure that all fuel-burning equipment and appliances are properly maintained and vented to the outside.

5. Workers should be encouraged to use CO detectors in areas where fuel-burning appliances are used or stored.

6. Vehicles should never run in enclosed spaces, such as garages or loading docks, and exhaust fumes should be vented outside.

7. Employers should provide adequate ventilation in areas where fuel-burning equipment or vehicles are used and monitor CO levels regularly.

8. Workers should be advised to take breaks and get fresh air if they feel lightheaded or dizzy while working with fuel-burning equipment.

9. Emergency procedures for CO exposure should be communicated to workers, including evacuation and medical attention.

10. Employers should promote a culture of safety around CO exposure and encourage workers to report any concerns or symptoms of CO exposure immediately.

7. Chemical Handling & Storage

1. Workers should be trained on proper handling and storing chemicals, including reading and understanding Material Safety Data Sheets (MSDS).

2. Chemicals should be appropriately labeled and stored in designated secured and locked areas when not in use.

3. Chemicals should be stored away from incompatible substances, such as oxidizers, and in a well-ventilated area.

4. Proper personal protective equipment (PPE) should be worn when handling chemicals, including gloves, goggles, and respirators.

5. Use appropriate spill response materials and procedures to clean chemical spills immediately.

6. Workers should avoid eating or drinking in areas where chemicals are being handled or stored.

7. Smoking should be prohibited where chemicals are being handled or stored.

8. Workers should be trained on the proper disposal of chemicals, including safely identifying and disposing of hazardous waste.

9. Emergency procedures for chemical spills and exposures should be communicated to workers, including evacuation and medical attention.

10. Employers should regularly inspect and maintain chemical storage areas and equipment to ensure they are in good condition and comply with safety regulations.

8. Cleaning Chemical Safety

1. Always read the label and follow the instructions when using cleaning chemicals.

2. When handling cleaning chemicals, use personal protective equipment (PPE) such as gloves, goggles, and a respirator mask.

3. Store cleaning chemicals in their original containers and keep them in a locked, well-ventilated area away from children and pets.

4. Never mix different cleaning chemicals, creating toxic fumes and dangerous reactions.

5. Dispose of cleaning chemicals following local regulations, and never pour them down the drain or into the trash.

6. Keep a first aid kit and emergency phone numbers nearby in case of accidental exposure to cleaning chemicals.

7. Ventilate the area when using cleaning chemicals to minimize exposure to fumes.

8. Use caution when transporting cleaning chemicals, and make sure they are adequately secured in the vehicle.

9. Train employees on the safe use and handling of cleaning chemicals, including proper disposal procedures.

10. Regularly inspect cleaning equipment and containers for signs of damage or leaks, and replace or repair as needed.

9. Cold & Flu Prevention

1. Wash your hands frequently with soap and water for at least 20 seconds, especially after touching common surfaces and before eating or touching your face.

2. Cover your mouth and nose when coughing or sneezing with a tissue or the inside of your elbow.

3. Avoid close contact with people who are sick, and stay home if you are sick.

4. Clean and disinfect frequently touched objects and surfaces such as doorknobs, keyboards, and phones regularly.

5. Use a hand sanitizer with at least 60% alcohol if soap and water are not readily available.

6. Practice good respiratory hygiene by using a mask around others if you have any cold or flu symptoms.

7. Stay hydrated and maintain a healthy diet, which can boost your immune system.

8. Get adequate sleep, which can also help support your immune system.

9. Avoid touching your face, especially your mouth, nose, and eyes, as germs can enter your body through these areas.

10. Consider getting vaccinated against the flu to protect yourself and those around you.

10. Computer Safety

1. Use strong passwords, change them regularly, and use two-factor authentication whenever possible.

2. Keep your operating system and all software up to date with the latest security patches and updates.

3. Install reputable antivirus and anti-malware software and keep it up to date.

4. Be wary of suspicious emails and attachments, and do not click on links or download files from unknown sources.

5. Use a firewall to block unauthorized access to your computer and network.

6. Back up important data regularly and store it in a secure location, such as an external hard drive or cloud storage.

7. Avoid using public Wi-Fi networks for sensitive activities such as banking or shopping, as these networks are often unsecured and vulnerable to hacking.

8. Be cautious when sharing personal information online, and only provide it to trusted websites and services.

9. Use a virtual private network (VPN) when accessing the internet from public networks or working remotely to encrypt your internet traffic.

10. Teach children safe online behavior and monitor their internet use to protect them from online predators and inappropriate content.

11. Confined Space Entry

1. Conduct a thorough risk assessment before entering a confined space. Identify potential hazards such as lack of oxygen, toxic gases, combustible materials, and physical obstructions.

2. Develop a safe work plan before entering the confined space. The plan should identify the tasks to be performed, the equipment needed, and the procedures for entry, work, and exit.

3. Train and equip all workers involved in confined space entry. Workers should be trained in hazard recognition, the proper use of personal protective equipment (PPE), and emergency response procedures.

4. Assign a competent attendant to monitor the entry and exit of workers. The attendant should be trained in the hazards of confined spaces and have the authority to stop work if necessary.

5. Ventilate the confined space before entering to remove any hazardous gases and provide workers fresh air.

6. Test the air quality in the confined space before entry and continuously monitor it while work is being performed.

7. Use appropriate PPE, including respirators, harnesses, lifelines, and gas detectors, as required by the job and the hazards present.

8. Use a permit system to ensure all necessary safety measures are in place before entry. All parties involved in the entry should review and sign the permit.

9. Establish effective communication between workers inside and outside the confined space. Use radios, hand signals, or other means to maintain contact and monitor the safety of workers.

10. Develop and rehearse an emergency response plan in case of an incident. The plan should include procedures for rescue, evacuation, and medical assistance.

12. CPR

1. Ensure that the scene is safe before starting CPR. Make sure there is no danger to yourself or the victim, and call for emergency services if necessary
.

2. Check for responsiveness by tapping the victim's shoulder and asking if they are okay. If there is no response, call for emergency services immediately.

3. Open the airway by tilting the victim's head and lifting their chin. Check for breathing by placing your ear near the victim's mouth and nose while looking for chest movement.

4. If the victim is not breathing, start chest compressions. Place the heel of one hand on the center of the victim's chest and your other hand on top of the first. Press down firmly and quickly, about 2 inches deep, at 100 to 120 compressions per minute.

5. If the victim has an obstructed airway, perform the Heimlich maneuver. Stand behind the victim and wrap your arms around their waist. Place a fist with one hand above the victim's navel. Grasp your fist with your other hand and press upward with a quick thrust,

6. If an Automated External Defibrillator (AED) is available, use it immediately. Follow the instructions on the device carefully.

7. Do not stop CPR until emergency medical services arrive or the victim starts breathing independently.

8. If there are other people around, assign specific roles to each person. One person should call for emergency services, one person should get the AED if available, and one person should continue performing chest compressions.

9. Stay calm and focused while performing CPR. Remember that you are helping to save someone's life.

10. Once emergency services arrive, please provide them with all the information they need about the victim's condition and the steps you have taken to perform CPR.

13. Crane Safety

1. Training: Ensure that all crane operators and workers have received appropriate training in crane safety, including proper operation, maintenance, and inspection procedures.

2. Inspection: Conduct daily pre-operational inspections of the crane, looking for any signs of wear, damage, or malfunction that could compromise safety. Regularly scheduled maintenance should also be performed.

3. Capacity: Understand the crane's rated capacity, and ensure loads do not exceed it. Overloading a crane can cause it to tip over, drop the load, or malfunction.

4. Stability: Maintain the crane's stability by ensuring it is level and that the outriggers or stabilizers are properly deployed. Use caution when operating on soft or uneven ground.

5. Communication: Establish clear communication procedures between the crane operator and workers on the ground. Use hand signals or radios to ensure everyone is on the same page.

6. PPE: Ensure that all workers wear the appropriate personal protective equipment (PPE), such as hard hats and safety glasses, when working near the crane.

7. Clearance: Ensure the crane has adequate clearance from overhead power lines and other obstructions. Maintain a safe distance from other equipment and workers.

8. Rigging: Properly rig the load using appropriate slings, hooks, and attachments. Check that the load is secure and balanced before lifting it.

9. Weather: Be aware of the weather conditions, including wind and lightning, and avoid operating the crane in hazardous conditions.

10. Emergency Procedures: Have an emergency plan in case of an accident or malfunction. Workers should know how to shut down the crane and evacuate the area if necessary.

14. Cuts & Abrasions Prevention

1. Wear protective clothing: Wearing appropriate clothing, such as long-sleeved shirts, pants, and closed-toe shoes, can help prevent cuts and abrasions.

2. Safety equipment: When working with sharp tools or machinery, use safety equipment such as gloves, goggles, and helmets to prevent injuries.

3. Keep work areas clean and organized: A clean and organized work area can prevent trips and falls, resulting in cuts and abrasions.

4. Use caution when handling sharp objects: Always handle sharp objects with care, and avoid rushing or cutting corners.

5. Use proper technique: When using sharp tools, use proper technique and always cut away from your body.

6. Keep tools sharp: Dull tools can slip and cause injuries, so keep your tools sharp and in good condition.

7. Use caution when working with chemicals: Chemicals can cause skin irritation and burns, so wear appropriate protective gear and handle them carefully.

8. Know your limits: Don't attempt tasks beyond your skill level, as this can increase the risk of injury.

9. Take breaks: Fatigue can increase the risk of accidents, so take regular breaks and avoid working long periods without rest.

10. Seek medical attention for serious injuries: If you sustain a severe cut or abrasion, seek medical attention promptly to prevent infection and promote proper healing.

15. Dealing with Chemical Spills

1. Safety first: Before dealing with a chemical spill, it is crucial to ensure your safety and the safety of others in the surrounding area. If the spill is significant or poses an immediate threat, evacuate the area and call for professional help.

2. Identify the chemical: It is essential to identify the spilled chemical to determine the appropriate cleanup procedure and necessary protective equipment. If available, consult the material safety data sheet (MSDS) for the specific chemical.

3. Contain the spill: Try to prevent the spill's spread by creating a barrier around the affected area, using sandbags, absorbent materials, or barriers. Do not allow the spilled chemical to enter drains, sewers, or bodies of water.

4. Wear appropriate protective equipment: Wear appropriate personal protective equipment (PPE) when cleaning up a chemical spill. PPE may include gloves, goggles, respirators, and protective clothing.

5. Ventilate the area: Ensure the area is well-ventilated to reduce the risk of inhalation of harmful vapors or fumes.

6. Neutralize the spill: Use appropriate spill kits or absorbents to neutralize or absorb the spilled chemical, following the manufacturer's instructions.

7. Collect and dispose of waste properly: Collect the contaminated materials and dispose of them following local regulations and the MSDS for the chemical.

8. Decontaminate the area: The site should be decontaminated using appropriate cleaning agents once the spill is cleaned up.

9. Notify appropriate personnel: Report the spill to the appropriate personnel, including your supervisor, the safety officer, and any emergency response teams.

10. Review and learn: Review the incident to identify areas for improvement and incorporate lessons learned into future spill response plans. Regular training and drills can help prepare personnel for potential spills.

16. Driving Accident Prevention

1. Follow traffic laws and regulations: Obey traffic signs and signals, speed limits, and other traffic laws. This can help prevent accidents caused by reckless driving.

2. Avoid distractions while driving: Distracted driving, such as texting or talking on the phone, eating or drinking, or adjusting the radio or navigation system, can lead to accidents. Stay focused on the road and avoid any distractions.

3. Maintain a safe distance from other vehicles: Keep a safe distance from the vehicle in front of you, especially in heavy traffic or bad weather. This will give you more time to react if the other vehicle stops or slows down suddenly.

4. Keep your vehicle maintained: Regularly maintain your vehicle, including checking tire pressure, brakes, lights, and other essential components. A well-maintained vehicle is less likely to break down or cause an accident.

5. Wear your seatbelt: Always wear your seatbelt while driving or riding in a vehicle. Seatbelts can significantly reduce the risk of injury or death in the event of an accident.

6. Avoid driving under the influence: Never drive while under the influence of alcohol or drugs. These impair your ability to drive safely and can lead to accidents.

7. Use your turn signals: Use your turn signals to indicate your intentions when turning or changing lanes. This can help other drivers anticipate your movements and avoid collisions.

8. Pay attention to pedestrians and cyclists: Be aware of pedestrians and cyclists on the road, especially in busy areas such as school zones or residential areas. Give them enough space and time to cross safely.

9. Avoid driving when fatigued: Driving while tired can be just as dangerous as driving under the influence. Make sure to get enough rest before getting behind the wheel.

10. Take a defensive driving course: Consider taking a defensive driving course to improve your driving skills and learn how to avoid accidents. These courses can also help lower your insurance premiums.

17. Dust Hazards

1. Dust is a significant safety hazard in many industries, including woodworking, metalworking, mining, and agriculture.

2. Combustible dust is hazardous, as it can ignite and cause explosions, leading to property damage, injury, and loss of life.

3. Employers should implement a dust hazard analysis to identify potential hazards and implement appropriate safety measures.

4. Safety measures may include dust collection systems, wet cleaning methods, and explosion suppression systems.

5. Regular inspections and maintenance of equipment and ventilation systems can prevent dust buildup and reduce the risk of fires and explosions.

6. Employees should receive training on safe work practices and the potential hazards of dust exposure.

7. When working with or near dust, workers should wear appropriate personal protective equipment (PPE), such as respirators and goggles.

8. Employers should establish an emergency response plan in case of a dust-related incident, including evacuation procedures and communication protocols.

9. Regular air quality testing can help identify potential dust hazards and allow for appropriate safety measures.

10. Employers should stay up-to-date on industry best practices and regulatory requirements for dust hazard safety.

18. Electrical Safety

1. Always turn off the power supply before working on any electrical equipment or wiring. This can prevent electrical shocks and other accidents.

2. When working with electrical systems, use appropriate electrical protective equipment such as gloves, goggles, and insulated tools.

3. Avoid using damaged or frayed electrical cords or cables. Damaged wires can expose you to electrical hazards such as shocks or fires.

4. Ensure that electrical cords are placed safely to prevent tripping hazards. This can prevent accidents in the workplace or at home.

5. Keep water and other liquids away from electrical equipment or wiring. Water can conduct electricity and can result in shocks or other hazards.

6. Do not overload electrical outlets. Overloaded circuits can result in fires, electrical shocks, or equipment damage.

7. Use appropriate voltage levels and fuses for electrical equipment. Using inappropriate voltage or fuses can result in equipment damage or electrical hazards.

8. Keep electrical equipment and wiring away from flammable or combustible materials. Sparks from electrical equipment can ignite these materials and cause fires.

9. Avoid touching electrical equipment or wiring with wet hands or while standing on a wet surface. Wet conditions can increase the risk of electrical hazards.

10. Regularly inspect and maintain electrical equipment and wiring to ensure safety and functionality. Faulty electrical systems can cause fires, equipment damage, or other hazards.

19. Ergonomics

1. Ergonomics is the study of designing equipment, tools, and workspaces to fit human physical and cognitive capabilities.

2. The primary goal of ergonomics is to optimize human performance, safety, and comfort in the workplace, thereby reducing the risk of injury, fatigue, and stress-related illnesses.

3. The principles of ergonomics apply to a wide range of industries, including manufacturing, healthcare, transportation, construction, and office work.

4. Ergonomics considers the physical dimensions of the human body, such as height, weight, reach, and range of motion, as well as cognitive factors, such as attention, memory, and decision-making.

5. Good ergonomic design considers individual and group needs, considering the workforce's diversity and the demands of different job tasks.

6. Key ergonomic factors impacting worker safety and comfort include lighting, noise, temperature, air quality, and posture.

7. Workplace design should allow for easy adjustability of equipment and tools to accommodate different body sizes and work styles.

8. Ergonomic training is essential for employees to recognize potential hazards and adopt safe work practices.

9. Ergonomic assessments of the workplace should be conducted regularly to identify potential hazards and implement solutions to improve safety and comfort.

10. The benefits of good ergonomic design include improved worker productivity, reduced absenteeism and turnover, and lower healthcare costs associated with workplace injuries and illnesses.

20. Fatigue Management

1. Prioritize Sleep: Getting enough sleep is crucial to combat fatigue. Adults should aim to get at least 7-8 hours of sleep per night.

2. Manage Workload: Overworking or taking on too many responsibilities can lead to burnout and fatigue. Prioritize tasks and delegate duties when possible.

3. Take Breaks: Regular breaks can help reduce mental and physical fatigue. Consider taking short walks, stretching or doing breathing exercises.

4. Stay Hydrated: Dehydration can cause fatigue, so drinking enough water throughout the day is essential.

5. Eat a Balanced Diet: Eating a balanced diet can help maintain energy levels throughout the day. Focus on foods high in protein, fiber, and complex carbohydrates.

6. Exercise Regularly: Regular exercise can help increase energy levels and reduce fatigue. Aim for at least 30 minutes of exercise most days of the week.

7. Practice Stress Management: Chronic stress can lead to fatigue. Consider practicing meditation, yoga, or deep breathing exercises to help manage stress.

8. Avoid Caffeine and Alcohol: While caffeine and alcohol may provide temporary energy boosts, they can also interfere with sleep quality and cause dehydration.

9. Seek Help for Sleep Disorders: If you are experiencing persistent fatigue despite getting enough sleep, you may have a sleep disorder such as sleep apnea. Speak with your healthcare provider for evaluation and treatment.

10. Prioritize Self-Care: Taking care of yourself is essential for managing fatigue. Make time for hobbies, relaxation, and activities that bring you joy and reduce stress.

21. Fire Prevention

1. Install Smoke Alarms: Smoke alarms are an essential part of fire prevention. Install smoke alarms on every level of your home and near sleeping areas.

2. Regularly Test Smoke Alarms: Test your smoke alarms at least once a month to ensure they work correctly.

3. Replace Old Batteries: Replace the batteries in your smoke alarms at least once a year or when you hear the low-battery warning.

4. Keep Fire Extinguishers: Keep at least one fire extinguisher on every level of your home, and learn how to use them properly.

5. Create a Fire Escape Plan: Create a fire escape plan with your family and practice it regularly. Make sure everyone knows two ways out of every room.

6. Keep Flammable Materials Away from Heat Sources: Keep flammable materials such as curtains, paper, and cleaning supplies away from heat sources such as stoves and heaters.

7. Don't Overload Electrical Outlets: Don't overload electrical outlets or extension cords. Use surge protectors to protect your electronics.

8. Don't Leave Cooking Unattended: Never leave cooking food unattended on the stove. Keep flammable materials away from the stove while cooking.

9. Don't Smoke Indoors: Smoking is a leading cause of home fires. Never smoke indoors, and properly dispose of cigarette butts.

10. Be Mindful of Candles: Candles can be a fire hazard if left unattended. Keep candles away from flammable materials and blow them out before leaving the room or going to bed.

22. First Aid

1. First aid is the initial assistance provided to a person who has been injured or suddenly taken ill before professional medical help arrives.

2. The primary objective of first aid is to preserve life, prevent the condition from worsening, and promote recovery.

3. It is essential to remain calm and composed when providing first aid. Panic can worsen the situation and increase the risk of injury to both the patient and the first aider.

4. The first step in providing first aid is to assess the situation and ensure it is safe for the first aider and the patient.

5. If the patient is unconscious, check their airway, breathing, and circulation. Start cardiopulmonary resuscitation (CPR) immediately if any of these are absent.

6. If the patient is conscious, introduce yourself and ask for their permission to help. Ensure that they are comfortable and help them into a comfortable position.

7. The ABC rule of first aid is Airway, Breathing, and Circulation. These are the most critical aspects of checking on any patient.

8. Basic first-aid techniques include bandaging, applying pressure to stop bleeding, immobilizing fractures or dislocations, and providing pain relief.

9. First aid kits should be kept in easily accessible locations and regularly checked and replenished.

10. It is essential to seek professional medical help as soon as possible, even if the patient appears stable. First aid is only a temporary measure and cannot replace medical treatment.

23. Foot Protection

1. Choose the proper footwear: Wearing the correct type of footwear for the job is essential. Ensure that your footwear provides good support, has slip-resistant soles, and is comfortable.

2. Inspect your footwear regularly: Before putting on your shoes, inspect them for any damage, such as cuts, holes, or loose soles. If you notice any damage, replace your footwear immediately.

3. Wear steel-toed boots for heavy-duty work: Steel-toed boots can provide extra protection for your toes and are recommended for heavy-duty work, such as construction or industrial jobs.

4. Use foot guards when necessary: Foot guards can be worn over your shoes to provide additional protection from falling objects or heavy machinery.

5. Keep your work area clean and tidy: A clean and organized work area can help prevent accidents and injuries to your feet.

6. Use caution when operating machinery: Be sure to follow all safety protocols when operating machinery that could potentially harm your feet.

7. Wear appropriate socks: Wearing socks that provide cushioning and support can help prevent blisters, corns, and other foot injuries.

8. Take breaks: Take regular breaks to rest your feet and stretch your legs, especially if you have to stand or walk for extended periods.

9. Stay alert: Be aware of your surroundings and potential hazards that could cause foot injuries.

10. Seek medical attention if necessary: If you experience a foot injury, seek medical attention to prevent further damage or complications.

24. H$_2$S Safety

1. H$_2$S (Hydrogen sulfide) is a colorless, flammable, and highly toxic gas with a characteristic odor of rotten eggs. It can cause serious health effects and even death at high concentrations.

2. H$_2$S is commonly found in the oil and gas industry, wastewater treatment plants, and other industrial processes. It can also be produced naturally in swamps, sewage systems, and some organic environments.

3. To ensure safety when working with H$_2$S, it is essential to identify and assess potential exposure sources, including monitoring and detecting the gas in the air.

4. Personal protective equipment (PPE), such as gas masks, respirators, and protective clothing, should be worn when working in areas where H$_2$S may be present.

5. Proper ventilation and air circulation are critical in preventing H$_2$S exposure. Employers should ensure that work areas are adequately ventilated and that air quality is monitored.

6. H$_2$S can be detected using various methods, including gas detection instruments, indicator tubes, and electronic detectors.

7. Emergency procedures should be established and communicated to all workers in the event of an H$_2$S release or exposure. Workers should know how to respond quickly and effectively, including evacuating the area and seeking medical attention.

8. H$_2$S is heavier than air, so that it can accumulate in low-lying areas, such as pits, trenches, and basements. These areas should be adequately ventilated and monitored for H$_2$S levels.

9. Proper handling and storage of chemicals and materials that can produce H$_2$S, such as sulfuric acid and organic matter, can help prevent H$_2$S exposure.

10. Regular training and education on H$_2$S safety should be provided to workers to ensure they are aware of the hazards associated with H$_2$S and how to prevent exposure.

25. Hand Injury Prevention

1. Wear appropriate protective gear: When working with machinery or performing tasks that could result in hand injury, wear gloves, goggles, and any other protective equipment necessary to keep your hands safe.

2. Use proper technique: Make sure you use proper technique when performing tasks such as lifting heavy objects, using hand tools, or typing on a keyboard to avoid repetitive stress injuries.

3. Take breaks during repetitive tasks can help prevent overuse injuries such as carpal tunnel syndrome.

4. Keep your work area clean: Keeping your work area clean and free of clutter can help prevent accidents and injuries.

5. Avoid distractions: When using hand tools or machinery, avoid distractions such as talking on the phone or watching TV, which can lead to accidents.

6. Be aware of your surroundings: Ensure you know your surroundings and the potential hazards in your work area.

7. Use tools and equipment properly: Follow instructions carefully when using hand tools or machinery to prevent accidents and injuries.

8. Stay focused: Stay focused on the task and avoid rushing or taking shortcuts, which can lead to accidents.

9. Use caution when handling chemicals: Wear gloves and follow proper safety procedures to avoid chemical burns or other injuries.

10. Seek medical attention for injuries: If you sustain an injury to your hand, seek medical attention immediately to prevent further damage and ensure proper healing.

26. Hand Tool Safety

1. Wear appropriate personal protective equipment (PPE) such as safety glasses, gloves, and hearing protection.

2. Inspect hand tools before each use for damage or wear and replace any worn or damaged tools.

3. Use the right tool for the job and ensure it is the correct size and type for the task.

4. Maintain a firm grip on the tool and keep your fingers away from the point of impact or blade.

5. Never use a tool with a loose or damaged handle, as it can cause injury or break during use.

6. Avoid using rusty or corroded tools, as they can weaken over time and break during use.

7. Use tools in a well-lit and well-ventilated area to avoid accidents due to poor visibility or fumes.

8. Never leave tools unattended or in a position where they could be knocked over and cause injury or damage.

9. Store tools in a designated area and keep them clean and dry to prevent rust and corrosion.

10. Always follow the manufacturer's instructions for properly using and maintaining hand tools.

27. Hard Hats

1. Hard hats are essential safety gear worn to protect the head from impact and penetration injuries on construction sites or any other workplace with a head injury risk.

2. The hard hat is designed to absorb the force of an impact and distribute it evenly over the surface of the hard hat, thus reducing the severity of the injury.

3. Hard hats come in different types and classes depending on the level of protection needed. Type 1 hard hats protect against impacts from above, while type 2 hard hats protect against impacts from both above and on the sides.

4. The hard hat class refers to its electrical protection level. Class G hard hats protect against low-voltage electrical hazards, Class E hard hats protect against high-voltage electrical hazards, and Class C hard hats provide no electrical protection.

5. Workers should inspect their hard hats regularly for signs of damage, wear, or deterioration. If any defects are found, the hard hat should be replaced immediately.

6. Hard hats should be properly fitted and adjusted to ensure a secure and comfortable fit. A loose or improperly fitting hard hat can fall off or shift during work, leading to injury.

7. Hard hats should be worn whenever there is a risk of head injury, even if the work is only for a short duration. This includes activities such as welding, grinding, or using power tools.

8. Workers should also wear other appropriate personal protective equipment (PPE) and hard hats, such as safety glasses, face shields, earplugs, or earmuffs, depending on the hazards present.

9. Employers are responsible for providing workers with appropriate PPE, including hard hats, and ensuring that they are trained on their proper use and maintenance.

10. Hard hats are an important component of workplace safety, but they are only one part of an effective safety program. Employers should also implement engineering controls, administrative controls, and safe work practices to eliminate or minimize hazards in the workplace.

28. HazMat Handling & Storage

1. HazMat, short for hazardous materials, are substances or materials that can cause harm to human health, property, or the environment. These include chemicals, gases, explosives, radioactive materials, and infectious substances.

2. Proper handling and storage of HazMat is crucial to prevent accidents, injuries, and environmental damage. HazMat should always be handled and stored by trained and qualified personnel who are familiar with the risks and hazards associated with the materials.

3. HazMat should be stored in a secure area designated for hazardous materials storage. The storage area should be properly ventilated and have adequate lighting. The storage containers should be labeled appropriately and have a secure lid to prevent spills and leaks.

4. The storage area should be located away from heat, flame, and ignition sources and should be designed to contain spills and leaks. The storage containers should be kept away from incompatible materials that could react with the HazMat.

5. HazMat should always be handled with proper personal protective equipment (PPE), including gloves, eye protection, and respiratory protection. The PPE should be selected based on the specific HazMat being handled.

6. HazMat should be transported securely and safely. The vehicles should be properly labeled, and the HazMat should be properly packaged and secured to prevent spills and leaks during transportation.

7. HazMat spills or leaks should be immediately contained and cleaned up by trained personnel using proper techniques and equipment. The spill response plan should be clearly communicated to all personnel who may come into contact with HazMat.

8. HazMat should be disposed of properly following local, state, and federal regulations. Improper disposal of HazMat can result in environmental damage and potential health hazards.

9. Proper training and education on HazMat handling and storage should be provided to all personnel who may come into contact with these materials. This training should include proper handling techniques, emergency response procedures, and personal protective equipment use.

10. Regular inspections and maintenance of HazMat storage areas, containers, and equipment should be conducted to ensure proper function and prevent accidents and spills.

29. Heat Illness Prevention

1. Stay hydrated: Drinking plenty of water and electrolyte-rich fluids helps prevent dehydration, which can lead to heat illness.

2. Dress appropriately: Wear lightweight, light-colored, loose-fitting clothing that allows sweat to evaporate quickly and helps keep your body cool.

3. Take breaks in the shade or cool indoor areas: Take frequent breaks in a cool, shaded area to allow your body to cool down and prevent overheating.

4. Avoid strenuous activity during the hottest part of the day: Schedule physical activities for the cooler times, such as early morning or late evening.

5. Know the signs and symptoms of heat illness: Symptoms of heat illness can include headache, dizziness, nausea, confusion, and fatigue. If you experience these symptoms, move to a shaded area and seek medical attention.

6. Use fans or air conditioning: If possible, use fans or air conditioning to help cool down indoor areas.

7. Monitor the weather forecast: Stay informed about the weather forecast, especially during times of high heat and humidity.

8. Acclimate yourself to the heat: If you are not used to working or exercising in hot weather, gradually increase your exposure to heat and take frequent breaks until your body becomes acclimated.

9. Avoid alcohol and caffeine: Both alcohol and caffeine can dehydrate you, making you more susceptible to heat illness. Try to avoid them during times of high heat and humidity.

10. Check on others: Check on elderly neighbors, children, and pets during times of high heat and humidity. They may be more vulnerable to heat illness.

30. High Voltage Safety

1. High voltage is any voltage exceeding 1000 volts, and it poses a serious risk to human life.

2. Only approach high voltage equipment or installations if you are a trained and authorized personnel.

3. Always use proper personal protective equipment (PPE) when working with high-voltage equipment. This may include insulated gloves, boots, goggles, and a face shield.

4. Before starting any work on high-voltage equipment, ensure it is de-energized and locked out. Only authorized personnel should be allowed to perform the lockout/tagout procedures.

5. High-voltage equipment should be properly grounded and bonded to prevent electric shock hazards.

6. Never touch any exposed conductors or equipment while energized, even if you think it is insulated. High voltage can jump and arc through the air.

7. Always work with a buddy or have someone nearby to assist in an emergency.

8. Use insulated tools when working on high-voltage equipment. This includes insulated pliers, screwdrivers, and wire strippers.

9. Regularly inspect high voltage equipment for any signs of damage or wear, and ensure it is properly maintained.

10. Always follow established safety procedures and guidelines when working with high-voltage equipment. If in doubt, consult with a qualified electrical professional.

31. Horseplay at the Workplace

1. Horseplay in the workplace can create an unsafe work environment, leading to accidents and injuries.

2. It is essential to establish clear guidelines and rules against horseplay in the workplace to prevent incidents from occurring.

3. Horseplay can lead to disciplinary action, including termination if it violates company policy.

4. Employees who engage in horseplay may be seen as unprofessional and could damage their reputation in the workplace.

5. Horseplay can lead to decreased productivity and disruptions in the workplace, negatively impacting the company's bottom line.

6. Employers are responsible for creating a safe work environment, and allowing horseplay to occur can be a breach of that responsibility.

7. Horseplay can also create tension and discomfort among coworkers who feel uncomfortable or unsafe in such an environment.

8. In extreme cases, horseplay can lead to harassment or bullying, which can have severe consequences for both the victim and the perpetrator.

9. It is vital for employees to report any instances of horseplay to their supervisor or HR department to prevent further incidents from occurring.

10. By promoting a culture of respect and professionalism, employers can help prevent horseplay in the workplace and create a safer and more productive work environment for everyone.

32. Importance of Hydration

1. Improved cognitive function: Drinking enough water throughout the day helps to keep your brain hydrated, which in turn helps to improve cognitive function, including memory, concentration, and overall mental clarity.

2. Increased productivity: When adequately hydrated, you will have more energy and feel more alert, leading to increased productivity at work.

3. Reduced fatigue: Dehydration can cause fatigue, making it difficult to focus and stay on task. Staying hydrated can help reduce fatigue and energize you throughout the day.

4. Improved physical performance: Drinking water can help regulate body temperature and prevent cramping, improving physical performance and reducing the risk of injury.

5. Better mood: Dehydration can lead to irritability and anxiety while staying hydrated can help improve mood and reduce stress.

6. Improved digestion: Drinking enough water helps keep the digestive system functioning properly, improving overall health and well-being.

7. Reduced headaches: Dehydration can cause headaches and migraines while staying hydrated can help to reduce the frequency and severity of these symptoms.

8. Boosted immune system: Drinking water can help to flush toxins out of the body and support the immune system, which can help to reduce the risk of illness and improve overall health.

9. Better skin health: Staying hydrated can help to keep the skin looking healthy and radiant, reducing the risk of dryness, flakiness, and other skin problems.

10. Improved overall health: Drinking enough water is essential for overall health and well-being, helping prevent a range of health problems and ensuring that the body functions properly.

33. Job Hazard Analysis

1. Job Hazard Analysis (JHA) identifies potential hazards and risks associated with a particular job or task.

2. The primary goal of JHA is to identify potential hazards and eliminate or control them before an accident or injury occurs.

3. JHA involves breaking down a job into steps and analyzing each step for potential hazards.

4. Hazards include physical, chemical, biological, and ergonomic factors.

5. The analysis should consider the equipment and tools used, the work environment, and the workers' abilities and limitations.

6. JHA involves observing the job or task, interviewing workers, and reviewing incident reports to identify potential hazards.

7. JHA should be performed before a new job or task is performed and when equipment, procedures, or the work environment changes.

8. JHA should involve workers and supervisors to ensure that everyone knows potential hazards and how to control them.

9. JHA should result in written procedures or work instructions describing the job or task and its associated hazards.

10. JHA is a crucial part of an effective health and safety management system, and it can help organizations reduce injuries and illnesses, increase productivity, and comply with regulatory requirements.

34. Ladder Safety

1. Choose the right ladder for the job: The ladder should be appropriate for the task. Ensure that it's the correct height, weight capacity, and material.

2. Inspect the ladder before use: Check for cracks, bends, or other defects. Ensure all bolts, nuts, and screws are secure, and the feet are not damaged.

3. Set the ladder up correctly: Make sure it is on a stable and level surface and fully extended and locked in place.

4. Secure the ladder: The ladder should be secured at the top and bottom to prevent slipping or falling. Use a stabilizer or leveler if necessary.

5. Maintain three points of contact: Keep two hands and one foot or two feet and one hand on the ladder at all times.

6. Climb and descend carefully: Face the ladder and climb up and down slowly and carefully. Take your time with the process.

7. Don't overload the ladder: Only one person should use the ladder at a time and stay within the weight capacity of the ladder.

8. Use the ladder for its intended purpose: Don't use it as a platform or support for other equipment. Don't lean the ladder against another surface.

9. Don't work on the top rungs: Stay off the top three rungs of the ladder. They are not designed to support your weight.

10. Store the ladder properly: Store the ladder in a dry, secure place, away from heat sources and chemicals. Keep it locked up and out of reach of children.

35. Lockout Tagout

1. Lockout Tagout (LOTO) is a safety procedure to ensure that dangerous machines and equipment are properly shut off and cannot be restarted before maintenance or repairs are completed.

2. LOTO aims to protect workers from the unexpected release of energy from machines or equipment during servicing or maintenance, which could cause serious injury or death.

3. LOTO involves using locks and tags to physically isolate the energy source(s) of the machine or equipment being serviced or maintained and to communicate to workers that the machine or equipment is not to be operated until the lock and tag are removed.

4. The lockout tagout process typically involves six steps: preparation, shutdown, isolation, locking and tagging, stored energy release, and verification.

5. Preparation involves identifying the machines and equipment that require LOTO and developing a written procedure for implementing LOTO.

6. Shutdown involves turning off the machine or equipment and ensuring all employees are safely out of harm's way.

7. Isolation involves physically disconnecting the energy sources of the machine or equipment, such as electrical, hydraulic, or pneumatic power sources.

8. Locking and tagging involves securing the energy-isolating devices with locks and tags, which should be unique to each worker performing maintenance or servicing tasks.

9. Stored energy release involves releasing residual energy from the machine or equipment, which could pose a hazard during maintenance or servicing.

10. Verification involves checking that all energy sources have been isolated and that the machine or equipment cannot be restarted until the locks and tags have been removed by authorized personnel.

36. Manual Handling & Lifting

1. Manual handling and lifting refer to the process of moving objects or loads by hand without the use of any mechanical or automated equipment.

2. Improper manual handling and lifting techniques can result in serious injuries, such as strains, sprains, and back problems.

3. Before lifting any object, it is essential to assess the load's weight, size, and shape, as well as the environment and potential hazards.

4. When lifting, keeping the back straight, the feet shoulder-width apart, and the knees bent is important.

5. Use the leg muscles, rather than the back, to lift the load. Keep the load close to the body and use the arms to help support the weight.

6. Avoid twisting the back while lifting or carrying objects. Turn the entire body, rather than just the upper body, to change direction if necessary.

7. Use appropriate lifting aids, such as trolleys, dollies, or straps, to assist with heavy or awkward loads.

8. Take regular breaks during manual handling and lifting tasks to avoid fatigue, which can increase the risk of injury.

9. Seek assistance from colleagues or use mechanical lifting aids if the load is too heavy or awkward to lift safely.

10. Employers are legally responsible for providing adequate training and equipment to ensure that employees can lift and move loads safely and without risk of injury.

37. Medical Emergencies

1. Time is critical in a medical emergency, so acting quickly and calling for help immediately is essential. Dial the emergency services or your local emergency number immediately.

2. Always stay calm in a medical emergency, and do your best to reassure the person in distress. This can help them feel more relaxed and help them to breathe more easily.

3. If someone is unconscious, make sure that their airway is clear and that they are breathing. If necessary, start CPR and continue until medical help arrives.

4. If someone is bleeding severely, apply pressure to the wound with a clean cloth or towel. Elevate the affected area if possible to help reduce the flow of blood.

5. If someone is experiencing a heart attack, call emergency services immediately and encourage the person to sit or lie down in a comfortable position. Avoid giving them anything to eat or drink.

6. If someone has a seizure, try to protect them from injury by clearing the area around them and cushioning their head. Do not restrain them, and do not put anything in their mouth.

7. If someone is experiencing an allergic reaction, administer an EpiPen and call for emergency services. Make sure the person stays still and does not move around too much.

8. If someone is experiencing a stroke, remember the acronym FAST: Face, Arm, Speech, Time. Check for facial drooping, arm weakness, and difficulty speaking. Call emergency services immediately.

9. Call Poison Control or emergency services immediately if someone has been poisoned. Try to identify the substance and follow any instructions given to you by the medical professionals.

10. Call a crisis hotline or emergency services if someone is experiencing a mental health crisis. Remain calm, listen to the person, and avoid making judgments or assumptions about their situation.

38. Mobile Equipment Safety

1. Always wear appropriate personal protective equipment (PPE), including hard hats, safety glasses, gloves, and steel-toed boots when using mobile equipment.

2. Before operating any mobile equipment, ensure you are appropriately trained and authorized to use the equipment.

3. Inspect mobile equipment before each use to ensure it is in safe working condition. Check for any damage or malfunctions and report any problems to the appropriate personnel.

4. Follow all posted speed limits and traffic regulations when operating mobile equipment. Slow down and use caution when working in congested areas.

5. Maintain a safe distance from other vehicles and equipment when operating mobile equipment. Keep a lookout for pedestrians and other hazards.

6. Use caution when driving on uneven terrain or in hazardous conditions, such as in wet or icy weather. Adjust your speed accordingly and avoid sudden movements.

7. Use appropriate signals when operating mobile equipment, such as hand signals or flashing lights, to indicate your intentions to other workers and equipment operators.

8. Always park mobile equipment on level ground with the brakes applied, and the engine turned off. Use chocks or blocks to prevent the equipment from rolling.

9. Never modify or remove safety features or guards from mobile equipment. They are designed to protect you and others from injury.

10. Report any accidents or near misses involving mobile equipment immediately to your supervisor or safety representative.

39. Near Miss Reporting

1. Near miss reporting refers to reporting incidents or events that could have resulted in an accident or injury but fortunately did not.

2. The purpose of near-miss reporting is to identify potential hazards and prevent future incidents from occurring.

3. Near-miss reporting is essential to safety management systems used in many industries, including healthcare, aviation, and manufacturing.

4. Reporting near misses is an important step in creating a safety culture within an organization, as it encourages employees to be proactive in identifying and reporting potential hazards.

5. Management should encourage and support near-miss reporting, and employees should be trained on how to report incidents and what information to include in their reports.

6. Near-miss reports should be confidential, and employees should not be penalized for reporting incidents.

7. Near miss reporting should be followed up with investigations to determine the root cause of the incident and identify corrective actions that can be taken to prevent future incidents.

8. Near-miss reporting can lead to cost savings for organizations by identifying potential hazards before they result in accidents or injuries, which can be costly in terms of lost productivity, medical expenses, and legal fees.

9. Near-miss reporting can also improve employee morale and job satisfaction, demonstrating that management values their input and is committed to creating a safe work environment.

10. Finally, near-miss reporting should be seen as a continuous improvement process. Organizations should use the information gathered from near-miss reports to identify trends and improve their safety management systems.

40. Office Safety

1. Keep walkways clear and unobstructed: Ensure all walkways and aisles are free from boxes, cords, and other obstacles that could trip someone.

2. Properly store and label hazardous materials: Keep all dangerous materials and chemicals properly labeled, stored, and away from other materials that could cause a chemical reaction.

3. Maintain good housekeeping practices: Keep the office clean and organized to reduce the risk of accidents and falls.

4. Use proper lifting techniques: Use your legs and not your back to avoid injury when lifting heavy objects.

5. Properly maintain equipment: Ensure that all office equipment is in good working condition and that any repairs or maintenance are performed promptly.

6. Fire safety: Have working smoke detectors, fire alarms, and fire extinguishers in the office, and conduct regular fire drills to prepare employees for emergencies.

7. Electrical safety: To prevent electrical accidents, use surge protectors, ground fault circuit interrupters, and other safety devices.

8. Ergonomic safety: Ensure all chairs, desks, and other furniture are adjusted to the proper height and angle to prevent strain and injury.

9. Personal protective equipment (PPE): Provide appropriate PPE such as safety glasses, gloves, and hard hats when necessary.

10. Train employees on office safety: Educate employees on the proper safety procedures and practices to ensure a safe work environment.

41. Personal Protective Equipment

1. Personal Protective Equipment (PPE) is equipment designed to protect individuals from workplace hazards that can cause injury or illness.

2. PPE can include gloves, safety glasses, respirators, hard hats, and hearing protection.

3. The selection of appropriate PPE is based on the hazard type and the exposure level. Employers are responsible for providing their employees with the necessary PPE.

4. It is important to properly fit and maintain PPE to ensure it provides the intended protection. Employees should also be trained on how to use PPE properly.

5. PPE should be worn as a last line of defense and should not be relied upon as the primary method of controlling hazards.

6. PPE can only protect if it is used consistently and correctly.

7. PPE should be stored in a clean, dry location and inspected regularly for damage or wear.

8. Some industries have specific regulations regarding PPE, such as the construction industry, which requires workers to wear hard hats and steel-toed boots on job sites.

9. Employers should provide PPE free of charge to their employees and ensure that it is available in the appropriate sizes and styles for each employee.

10. PPE can help reduce workplace injuries and illnesses, but it should always be used with other safety measures, such as engineering and administrative controls.

42. Preventing Workplace Violence

1. Establish clear policies and procedures: Create and implement policies that address workplace violence. These policies should define unacceptable behavior, identify guidelines for reporting incidents, and outline the steps that will be taken to prevent and address violence.

2. Conduct background checks: Perform background checks on all employees before hiring. This can help to identify any past incidents of violence or other concerning behavior.

3. Provide training: Train employees to identify and prevent workplace violence. This training should include information on the warning signs of violent behavior, conflict resolution strategies, and reporting procedures.

4. Encourage open communication: Create an environment where employees feel comfortable reporting incidents of workplace violence or potential threats. Encourage open communication and allow employees to report concerns anonymously if they feel more comfortable doing so.

5. Implement security measures: Implement security measures such as access control, security cameras, and security personnel. These measures can help deter violent behavior and provide a quick response to an incident.

6. Foster a positive work culture: Foster a positive work culture that promotes respect, professionalism, and teamwork. This can help to prevent workplace conflicts and reduce the likelihood of violent behavior.

7. Offer employee support: Offer services such as counseling, employee assistance programs, or access to mental health resources. This can help employees manage stress and other issues leading to violent behavior.

8. Respond quickly and appropriately: Respond promptly and appropriately to any incidents of workplace violence. This may involve contacting law enforcement, providing medical assistance, or taking other steps to ensure the safety of employees.

9. Monitor high-risk employees: Monitor employees with a history of violent behavior or who have exhibited concerning behavior. This may involve additional training, counseling, or other interventions.

10. Continuously evaluate and improve: Continuously evaluate and improve workplace violence prevention policies and procedures. This may involve reviewing incident reports, seeking employee feedback, and updating policies and procedure.

43. Respiratory Protection

1. Respiratory protection refers to equipment or devices that protect the respiratory system from harmful airborne particles or contaminants.

2. Respiratory protection is essential for workers exposed to hazardous substances like dust, chemicals, and biological agents.

3. Respiratory protection devices include air-purifying respirators, which filter contaminants out of the air, and supplied-air respirators, which supply clean air from an external source.

4. The selection of the appropriate respiratory protection device depends on the hazard type and level and exposure duration and frequency.

5. Respiratory protection devices must be properly fitted to ensure a tight seal and maximum protection.

6. Proper maintenance and inspection of respiratory protection equipment are essential to ensure it functions effectively.

7. Training in properly using and caring for respiratory protection equipment is critical for all workers required to wear it.

8. Employers are responsible for providing workers with the necessary respiratory protection equipment and using it correctly.

9. In addition to workplace settings, respiratory protection may be necessary for certain activities, such as home renovation and outdoor activities in areas with poor air quality.

10. Respiratory protection is essential to a comprehensive occupational health and safety program. It should be integrated with other hazard control measures to ensure the safety and health of workers.

44. Scaffolding Safety

1. Proper Training: Workers should receive adequate training and instruction on safely using scaffolding before starting work.

2. Inspection: Scaffolding should be thoroughly inspected before use and periodically checked for defects or damage.

3. Stability: Scaffolds should be braced on a solid foundation to prevent movement or instability.

4. Weight Limits: Scaffolds should be designed to support the weight of the workers, materials, and equipment used on them.

5. Guardrails: Guardrails should be installed on all open sides and ends of scaffolding to prevent falls.

6. Personal Protective Equipment: Workers should wear appropriate personal protective equipment, such as hard hats, non-slip shoes, and harnesses, when working on scaffolding.

7. Proper Access: To prevent falls, scaffolds should have safe and secure access points, such as ladders or stairs.

8. Weather Conditions: Scaffolds should not be used during adverse weather conditions, such as high winds, heavy rain, or snow.

9. Communication: Proper communication between workers and supervisors ensures safe scaffold usage.

10. Maintenance: Scaffolds should be maintained regularly, and any damage or defects should be repaired or replaced immediately.

45. Slips, Trips & Falls

1. Slips, trips, and falls are a leading cause of workplace injuries and accidents.

2. Slips occur when there is a lack of traction between the foot and the walking surface, often due to spills, wet floors, or loose rugs.

3. Trips occur when a person's foot hits an object, causing them to lose their balance and potentially fall.

4. Falls can result from slips and trips, leading to serious injuries, such as broken bones, head injuries, and sprains.

5. Employers have a legal responsibility to provide a safe working environment and must take steps to prevent slips, trips, and falls.

6. This can include providing slip-resistant flooring, ensuring walkways are free of clutter and obstacles, and posting warning signs for hazardous areas.

7. Employees can also take steps to prevent slips, trips, and falls, such as wearing slip-resistant shoes and being aware of their surroundings.

8. Regular maintenance and cleaning can help prevent slips, trips, and falls by ensuring that walking surfaces are free of hazards.

9. In the event of a slip, trip, or fall, it's essential to report the incident to a supervisor and seek medical attention if necessary.

10. Prevention is vital regarding slips, trips, and falls, and both employers and employees must work together to create a safe working environment.

46. Stress Management

1. Prioritize your workload: Identify high-priority and urgent tasks, and tackle them first. Breaking down your tasks into smaller, more manageable steps can help you feel less overwhelmed.

2. Practice mindfulness: Take regular breaks to clear your mind and refocus your attention. Mindfulness meditation or deep breathing exercises can reduce stress and increase focus.

3. Regular exercise: Physical activity can help relieve stress and boost mood. Take a brisk walk during your lunch break, or find a workout buddy to motivate you.

4. Maintaining a healthy diet: Eating a balanced diet can help regulate mood and energy levels. Avoid sugary snacks and caffeine, which can cause a spike in energy followed by a crash.

5. Set realistic expectations: Be honest with yourself and your boss about what you can accomplish in a given time. Take on only what you can handle.

6. Communicate with coworkers: Building strong relationships can help create a supportive work environment. Feel free to ask for help when you need it.

7. Take time off: Everyone needs a break from work occasionally. Use your vacation days to recharge your batteries and return to work feeling refreshed.

8. Practice time management: Use tools like calendars and to-do lists to help you stay organized and on track. This can help reduce stress by giving you a clear plan of action.

9. Seek support: Don't hesitate to contact a therapist or other mental health professional if you're feeling overwhelmed or stressed.

10. Stay positive: Focus on the things that are going well in your work and personal life. Cultivate a sense of gratitude and try to maintain a positive outlook even during challenging times.

47. Trenching Safety

1. Conduct a thorough site assessment before digging a trench to identify potential hazards such as underground utilities, unstable soil, or nearby structures.

2. Ensure that all workers are trained and experienced in trenching safety and provide them with the necessary personal protective equipment (PPE), such as hard hats, gloves, and safety glasses.

3. Keep the trench as narrow as possible to reduce the risk of collapse. The maximum allowable width is typically two feet for trenches less than five feet deep.

4. Always slope the sides of the trench or install shoring, shielding, or other protective systems to prevent cave-ins.

5. Maintain a safe distance from heavy equipment operating near the trench to prevent accidental contact or collapse.

6. Be aware of the dangers of trench foot, a painful condition caused by prolonged exposure to wet and cold conditions. Provide workers with appropriate footwear and ensure they take frequent breaks in warm and dry locations.

7. Keep the trench clear of water, debris, and other materials that can increase the risk of slips, trips, and falls.

8. Always use caution when entering or exiting the trench and ensure that ladders or other access systems are appropriately secured.

9. Ensure that all trenches are correctly backfilled and compacted after the work is complete to prevent settling or collapse.

10. Always have an emergency plan in case of an accident or injury, including a method of communication, first aid supplies, and procedures for contacting emergency services.

48. Truck & Trailer Safety

1. Regular Maintenance: Regular maintenance is crucial for truck and trailer safety. Check brakes, tires, lights, and other essential components before every trip.

2. Proper Loading: Loading is essential for truck and trailer safety. Always ensure the load is evenly distributed and correctly secured to prevent accidents.

3. Use Safety Equipment: Ensure you have the appropriate safety equipment, such as reflective vests, fire extinguishers, and emergency kits, in an emergency.

4. Check the Weather: Be aware of weather conditions before going. High winds, heavy rain, and snow can make driving dangerous.

5. Driver Training: Proper driver training is essential for truck and trailer safety. Drivers should be trained in handling the vehicle, including braking, cornering, and steering.

6. Driver Fatigue: Driver fatigue is a significant cause of accidents. Ensure that drivers get enough rest and take breaks as needed.

7. Know the Route: Knowing the route and potential hazards can help prevent accidents. Plan and be aware of construction zones, narrow roads, and steep inclines.

8. Check Blind Spots: Blind spots can be significant hazards for truck and trailer drivers. Always check blind spots before making a turn or changing lanes.

9. Speed Management: Speed management is crucial for truck and trailer safety. Always obey posted speed limits and adjust your speed based on road conditions.

10. Communication: Communication is essential for truck and trailer safety. Ensure that drivers have a way to communicate with other drivers, dispatchers, and emergency services.

49. Winter Driving

1. Slow down: Winter driving conditions require drivers to slow down due to reduced visibility and traction. It's essential to adjust your speed to the road conditions.

2. Prepare your vehicle: Make sure your vehicle is ready for winter driving by checking the battery, brakes, tires, and windshield wipers. Ensure your car has adequate snow and ice traction.

3. Keep a safe distance: Increase the distance between your vehicle and the one in front. This gives you more time to react to sudden stops or slippery conditions.

4. Use your headlights: In winter, visibility is reduced due to snow, fog, and early sunsets. Turn on your headlights to improve visibility and help other drivers see you.

5. Don't rely solely on technology: Although antilock brakes and traction control can help in winter driving, they must be more foolproof. It's important to drive defensively and use your judgment.

6. Watch out for black ice: Black ice is a thin, invisible layer of ice that can form on roads and cause slippery conditions. Slow down and be extra cautious when driving over bridges, overpasses, and shaded areas.

7. Be patient: Winter driving can be stressful, but staying calm and patient on the road is essential. Avoid sudden movements or overreacting to other drivers' mistakes.

8. Know how to handle a skid: If you encounter a skid, don't panic. Take your foot off the gas pedal and steer in the direction you want to go. Avoid slamming on the brakes, as this can make the skid worse.

9. Stay informed: Keep an eye on weather reports and traffic updates to stay knowledgeable about changing conditions. Avoid driving in hazardous weather conditions if possible.

10. Be prepared for emergencies: In case of an emergency, keep a winter survival kit in your car, including blankets, a flashlight, a first-aid kit, and extra food and water. Additionally, ensure your cell phone is fully charged before hitting the road.

50. Workplace Housekeeping

1. Good workplace housekeeping is essential for maintaining a safe and productive working environment.

2. Maintaining cleanliness and orderliness in the workplace by eliminating clutter, debris, and unnecessary materials.

3. A clean and organized workspace improves efficiency and productivity by reducing the time spent searching for tools, equipment, or materials.

4. Poor workplace housekeeping can lead to accidents and injuries, such as slips, trips, and falls.

5. It can also contribute to the spread of germs and bacteria, leading to illness and lost productivity.

6. All employees are responsible for maintaining good workplace housekeeping, not just custodial staff.

7. This includes keeping personal workspaces clean and organized and properly disposing trash and other waste materials.

8. Proper storage and labeling of hazardous materials is also critical for workplace safety.

9. Regular cleaning and maintenance of equipment and machinery are necessary to prevent accidents.

10. Employers should establish workplace housekeeping policies and provide training to ensure all employees understand the importance of maintaining a clean and safe working environment.

Safety Meeting Sign-In Sheet

Date: _____

Location: _____

Presented by: _____

Topic: _____

Print Name	Signature

Safety in 10
Safety Meeting Notes

Date: _____

Location: _____

Presented by: _____

Topic: _____

1. _____
_____
_____
_____
_____

2. _____
_____
_____
_____
_____

3. _____
_____
_____
_____
_____

4. _____
_____
_____
_____
_____

5. _____

6. _____

7. _____

8. _____

9. _____

10. _____

Safety in 10
Points Covered

Date: _____

Location: _____

Presented by: _____

Topic: _____

Point #	✓	Initials	Additional Discussion from Notes (Yes or No)
1			
2			
3			
4			
5			
6			
7			
8			
9			
10			

SafetyDownloaded.com

Visit our website to make your safety program as easy as clicking "download"

Training Videos
Safety Meeting Guides
Form Templates
Safety in 10 Book Series
& Much More